A Library Story

A Library STORY

Building a New Central Library

by Jennifer Vogel

Millbrook Press

Minneapolis

FOR LOGAN, my smarty-pants niece

The publisher wishes to thank: Kit Hadley, Bo Spurrier, Marcelyn Sletten, Terrance Roy Jr., Barbara Johnson, Sara Goodnough, Nina Ebbighausen, Jane Boss, Mary Kramer, Frank Hurley, Linda Loven, Natalie Hart, JoEllen Haugo, Charles Gimon, Walter Gegner, Karen Louise Boothe, Sally Westby, Colin Hamilton, Cesar Pelli, Bill Butler, Aicha Woods, Elijah Huge, Mig Halpine . . . and everyone else at the Minneapolis Public Library, the City of Minneapolis, and Pelli Clarke Pelli Architects, who so generously contributed to the making of this book.

Millbrook Press, Inc.
A division of Lerner Publishing Group
241 First Avenue North
Minneapolis, Minnesota 55401 U.S.A.

Website address: www.lernerbooks.com

Library of Congress Cataloging-in-Publication Data

Vogel, Jennifer.
    A library story: building a new central library / by Jennifer Vogel.
       p.   cm.
    Includes bibliographical references and index.
    ISBN-13: 978-0-8225-5916-0 (lib. bdg. : alk. paper)
    ISBN-10: 0-8225-5916-1 (lib. bdg. : alk. paper)
    1. Library buildings—Minnesota—Minneapolis—Design and construction—Juvenile literature. 2. Public libraries—Minnesota—Minneapolis—Juvenile literature. 3. New Central Library (Minneapolis, Minn.)—Juvenile literature. I. Title.
Z679.2.U54V64 2007
727'.8'09776579—dc22   2005023742

Manufactured in the United States of America
1 2 3 4 5 6 – DP – 12 11 10 09 08 07

In any Library in the world, I AM AT HOME

—writer Germaine Greer

OMAHA PUBLIC LIBRARY
215 SOUTH 15 STREET, OMA
Information
444-4800
24 Hou
I assume full responsib
all charges associate
notice of loss

DANBURY PUBL
(203) 7
170 M
DANB
www.

Minneapolis Public Library

Huntsville
Madison County
Public

er'e) n., pl. -ies. Abbr. lib.
rmation center with resources fo
2. A repository for literary an
such as books, periodicals
nlets, and prints kept for reading o
s
ally arranged for reference. 4. A
maintaining such a collection

BRARY CARD

SAN LEANDRO Public Library

The New York
Public Library
THE BRANCH LIBRARIES

A Letter from the Architect, Cesar Pelli

I love libraries. They can be magical places where many worlds await us. In our design of the Minneapolis Central Library, we tried to capture some of this magic and excitement. The building is enclosed in glass, letting light in and providing views out. Picking up a book and reading in this building is pure pleasure. In the evening, the library glows like a lantern.

The windows around the building have special designs on them. On the east side, the designs are birch trees, and on the west side, they are prairie grass. On the north, looking toward the Mississippi River, the designs show ripples on the water, and on the south side, they are heavy snow on tree branches.

The entrances to the building can be seen from far away because of shiny steel overhangs that project over the sidewalks. These overhangs are the ends of a long wing-shaped roof that covers Library Commons, the central space of the library. This is a tall, exciting space filled with light and people.

In the design, we were inspired by the spirit of Minneapolis. The building is beautiful and functional, restrained and exuberant, practical and poetic. It is a classical design that will look new for a very long time. It is a unique building for a unique city.

A Letter from the Library Director,

Kit Hadley

Welcome! I invite you to take a tour of the new Minneapolis Central Library in the pages of this book.

This library is the product of many people's imaginations. Minneapolis voters imagined a state-of-the-art library and a beautiful public gathering space. The architects, along with citizens and officials, envisioned a library that will accommodate the city's needs for years to come. Students from around the city helped design a teen library that is exclusively theirs.

The new Central Library is remarkable, but it has much in common with libraries across the country. What happens inside any library is the product of your imagination. What do you want to read? What do you want to write, compose, create, invent? Where in the universe do you want to explore? Your library is a place for you to read, listen to music, study with friends, organize a poetry slam, or just hang out.

Newcomers from other countries remind us of a truth sometimes taken for granted. The public library is a powerful place, based on a powerful idea. Because it belongs to everyone, the public library is part of our common wealth. The books and resources are free to all people. Differences among us are welcomed and celebrated.

After you finish reading, be sure to pay a visit to your own community's library. Come in and make it your own.

BOOM! CRASH!

LOOK OUT FOR THE WRECKING BALL!

The Minneapolis Central Library is coming down.

The workers pounded against the sides of the building. They smashed until there was nothing but rubble. What a mess! What did they do with all that old cement and metal? It didn't go into a garbage dump. Instead, almost all the materials from the building were recycled. The rubble became sidewalks, roads, and even other buildings. That's smart thinking—and libraries are known for good ideas. The library was torn down to make way for a brand-new Central Library in Minneapolis, Minnesota.

Downtown Minneapolis **has had a public library for more than one hundred years. The first one opened in 1889. It looked a lot like a castle.** A statue of Minerva—the Roman goddess of wisdom—was perched above the entrance. Minerva reminds people that libraries stand for knowledge and wisdom of all kinds. And the wisdom doesn't just come from books.

For example, the original library kept live animals, including a rattlesnake and a lizard called a Gila monster. It also had two real mummies from Egypt. People came from all over the state to see them.

As the years passed, the city changed. People needed new things from the library. And the library needed room for more books.

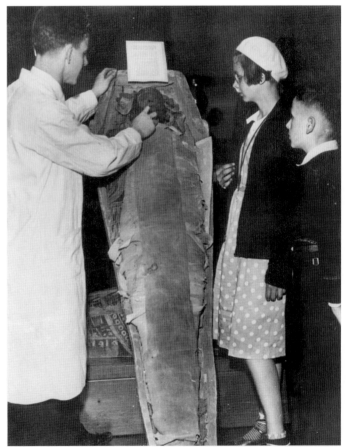

Keeping live animals in the library could be dangerous. In 1928, one of the animals bit the caretaker, Grace Wiley. She spent several days in the hospital!

More than 150,000 new books are published each year. But most libraries can't hold every book that comes out. How do librarians decide which books to buy? They look for those that will be the most useful and interesting to their patrons. Anybody who uses a library is called a patron.

Benjamin Franklin started a library in Philadelphia, Pennsylvania, in 1731. People had to pay to join the library. By 1741, the library had 375 books.

After seventy-two years, the first downtown Minneapolis library ran out of room. People said it was "bursting at the seams." So, in 1961, workers moved the books to a building six blocks away. This was downtown's second library. The statue of Minerva came along and so did the mummies. But the big attraction at the second library was its planetarium, a theater that presents shows about other planets and outer space. The first library had had a small planetarium, but the second one was much bigger. Inside the planetarium's shiny dome, adults and kids watched pictures of planets, stars, and galaxies moving through the night sky.

Over time, the Minneapolis Library's planetariums have attracted more than 4 million visitors.

The same year the new library opened, President John F. Kennedy gave an important speech. He said the United States would fly a person to the moon by the end of the 1960s. Everybody seemed excited about outer space. In Minneapolis, a ten-year-old boy named George "Pinky" Nelson visited the planetarium. He loved it. When he got older, he studied astronomy and became a NASA astronaut.

Pinky Nelson went on three spaceflights and logged 411 hours in space.

By 2000, the second downtown Minneapolis library could no longer do its job. The building was in bad shape. It was much too small for all the new books. Plus, the library had added something new: computers. Patrons use computers to search the library's catalog, to play games, and to browse on the Internet. The library also needed more space for DVDs, CDs, magazines, and government documents. It was ready for another new home.

A public library doesn't belong to the person in charge or to the librarians. It belongs to everybody. That's what it means to be a public place. So when the Minneapolis library decided it needed a new building, it had to ask the people of Minneapolis to pay for it. In 2000, the city held a vote, and the people said yes.

The Library of Congress, located in Washington, D.C., is the largest library in the world. It has more than 130 million items on about 530 miles of bookshelves.

City Council Member

Before construction could start, the library needed money.
Most of the money came from taxpayers. But taxpayers don't always want to pay higher taxes. That's why the Minneapolis Public Library Board and the Minneapolis City Council got involved. They helped educate people about why a new library would be a good use of their taxes.

Barb Johnson is on the city council. She was in favor of giving city money to the library. Barb has happy memories of visiting the library when she was a kid. Sometimes she went to the original downtown library—the one that looked like a castle. She especially remembers the mummies. Barb would also visit her neighborhood library. She was known for reading every children's book in the place. "I just loved going to the library," she said. "I was a real reader. My mother would catch me at night. I would be in bed reading by flashlight."

She believes education and access to information are very important. "Every great city should have a great library."

The total cost of the new Central Library was $125 million.

Minnesotans like to read and write. Some well-known authors come from or live in the state. F. Scott Fitzgerald was born in Saint Paul, Minnesota, in 1896. His most famous book is *The Great Gatsby*. Current writers Judith Guest and Louise Erdrich live in Minnesota. So do children's authors Kate DiCamillo, who wrote *Because of Winn-Dixie*, Pete Hautman, who wrote *Godless*, and Nancy Carlson, who writes and illustrates the Nancy Carlson's Neighborhood series.

When we read a book, we have to use our imaginations. Reading lets us travel to foreign countries, make-believe worlds, and even to outer space. We learn about people who are like us and others who are different. Libraries have books about people who have done all kinds of things. If you want to be a basketball star, an inventor, a fashion designer, or the president of the United States, the library has a book for you.

The new Central Library's auditorium has 243 chairs. Each chair has the name of a Minnesota author on it.

FROM THE GROUND UP

Many people had ideas about how to make the library the best it could be. These people included politicians, architects, urban planners, and ordinary citizens. Kids and teenagers had a chance to share their opinions too. All this information went to the people who were hired to create the new building.

Architect Cesar Pelli was the head designer for the new library. Pelli has designed buildings all over the world, including the Carnegie Hall Tower in New York City and the Petronas Towers in Kuala Lumpur, Malaysia. Pelli designed the new Minneapolis library to look good while still fitting in with the rest of the city. He also made sure that the building would be able to change as the library's needs changed. "We have built total flexibility into the building," Pelli said.

The Petronas Towers are 1,483 feet tall. When they were built in 1998, they were the tallest buildings in the world.

The United States has approximately 117,664 libraries. Of that number, 9,211 are public libraries. Many of the other libraries are at schools and universities.

The architects' finished plans—called blueprints—would give Minneapolis the largest library the city had ever had. Many more books could be placed on shelves instead of in storage rooms. Readers would be able to look through more books on their own. The new building would have room for hundreds of computers. The design also included a café, an auditorium, and meeting rooms. It was truly a design for a twenty-first-century library.

Cesar Pelli's first sketch for the new Central Library shows the overall shape and feeling he wanted the building to have.

After the architects had the blueprints ready, a wrecking crew tore down the old library. But before workers could start building the new library, they had to dig an enormous hole.

The hole was for an underground parking garage. That way, people coming to busy downtown Minneapolis wouldn't have to search for a parking place. The library is also near the light-rail train and many bus lines. A person doesn't need a car to get there. That's important, because many people don't own cars or don't like to drive.

The hole in the ground was about 300 feet wide by 300 feet long. The hole was 30 feet deep at the deepest point.

Workers poured thick cement into wooden molds along the edges of the parking garage to make walls. They formed cement pillars to support the building's weight. But they're not like the pillars in most buildings. Usually the cement for a pillar is poured into molds that are divided into sections. This leaves bumps all the way up. The library's pillars were made using larger molds for a more elegant appearance. The pillar surfaces are almost completely smooth. Workers placed the pillars in a pattern across the floor of the parking garage to hold up the building above.

There are 208 pillars in the parking garage and 674 in the library as a whole.

Behind the Scenes
Architect

The library had several architects. They worked together to design a building that all the city's residents could use. Nina Ebbighausen was especially excited to be part of such an important project. "It was a very passionate thing for me," she said. "I like designing for a social purpose."

The architects wanted to make the library as useful and welcoming as possible. They also wanted it to reflect the city's history. Because the Mississippi River winds its way along the edge of downtown Minneapolis, some of the city's streets come together at odd angles. The library is at one of those places where the block isn't really square. The building's design reflects that. Library Commons, the building's atrium, is shaped like a triangle.

No matter what happens in the future, Nina believes that we will always have books and that we'll always need libraries. And most important, we'll always need a place to gather. "We put in tall ceilings," she said, "and other things that make this feel like a grand, significant place. It deserves to be recognized as special."

The library's design plans were more than 16,000 pages long.

After the parking garage was finished, the project moved aboveground. Workers built wooden forms and lay them on top of the pillars. They poured cement into the forms to make enormous slabs.

These slabs, which are level with the street, created the roof of the parking garage and the ground floor of the library. The pillars hold up the slabs in the same way a table's legs hold up a tabletop. With more than one hundred construction workers on-site, the library rose quickly to a height of 105 feet.

The new Central Library is 355,000 square feet. That's the size of seventy-five basketball courts!

For the outside of the building, the architects chose interesting materials, such as Minnesota limestone. This yellowish rock forms in layers at the bottoms of rivers and lakes over many years. A close look at the stone reveals the lines from the layering.

The stone helps the library fit in with its surroundings. The limestone was cut from a mine in Mankato, a city southwest of Minneapolis and Saint Paul. Mankato's limestone is known for being strong and long lasting.

On an average day, workers could put up six or seven pieces of limestone.

Construction sites are busy places. Workers use heavy, dangerous machines. Everyone on the site—even visitors—had to wear hard hats and safety goggles. The company in charge of the construction planned everything carefully to avoid accidents. Workers in high places clipped on safety harnesses. The harnesses were attached to a secure place. If workers lost their balance, they wouldn't fall to the ground.

The workers also found other ways to stay safe. Every morning, they met to stretch and warm up their muscles. These exercises helped them get ready for the day's work.

The average hard hat weighs between 11 and 13 ounces. That's less than a hardcover copy of this book weighs.

The library is laid out in two halves, with a north wing and a south wing. The north wing holds most of the books, movies, and other materials for the public. To find a book, you need to know how a library is organized. Libraries arrange their books in a few different ways. Picture books and other fiction are in alphabetical order by the author's last name. That means a book by Roald Dahl would come before a book by Madeleine L'Engle.

For nonfiction books, some libraries use the Dewey decimal system. This system gives each book a number between 000 and 999. The number tells you what the book is about and where in the library you can find it. For example, all books that have to do with geography and history are between 900 and 999.

A man named Melvil Dewey created the Dewey decimal system in 1876.

The Minneapolis Central Library uses the Library of Congress (LC) system for nonfiction books. This system gives each book one or two letters followed by numbers. The letters tell you what the book is about. For example, all geography books have a LC code that starts with the letter *G*. If you need help looking up a book in the catalog or finding it on the shelves, you can always ask a librarian.

The best part about a library is that you can read all the books for free. Unlike bookstores, libraries don't charge you any money—as long as you bring your materials back on time. If you lose a book or return it late, you may have to pay a fine. Libraries use money from fines to help buy more books and to pay the library staff.

In 1968, an Ohio man returned a book that his great-grandfather had checked out in 1823. The fine was $22,646. Luckily, the library didn't make him pay!

Many cities, including Minneapolis, have tight budgets. The city cut the amount of money it gives to its libraries. As a result, Minneapolis libraries had to reduce the number of hours they are open. They also buy fewer books than they used to. Libraries need every penny they can get.

The south wing holds meeting rooms and other library services. Here you find the café, the bookstore, and the auditorium, Pohlad Hall. The south wing is also where the library staff fix damaged books. The library has its own bindery with special glues and papers. Experts in the bindery can take an old book that's falling apart and make it sturdy again. Then more people can borrow it. They also bind together magazine issues so they'll last longer.

The library binds and repairs as many as 20,000 books and magazines every year.

GLASS ALL AROUND

A large, airy space called Library Commons connects the two wings of the library. It's a good way to get from floor to floor or from one side of the building to the other. You can go by elevator, escalator, bridge, or stairway. But Library Commons is more than just a passageway. It is a meeting and greeting place. People here can sit or walk. They can stop to talk to friends. This is an important role for libraries. As cities become more spread out and people live farther from one another, it becomes harder to find places to gather. The other people at your library might be from your neighborhood or they might be from halfway around the world. The library helps people come together.

Public libraries in the United States have about 1.2 billion visitors each year.

Because Library Commons is a space for seeing and being seen, it is almost all glass. The walls are as tall as the building itself. A special sheet of glass called a curtain wall faces the street on the Nicollet Avenue side of the building. This glass wall does not support the weight of the building. It's made from thirty-two panes of special, extremely clear glass. Some of the panes are as large as 17 feet across and weigh as much as a small car. All this glass makes for wonderful views of downtown.

No company in the United States could craft glass big enough for the curtain wall. The glass panes had to be made in Austria.

The glass doesn't end at Library Commons. The table-and-legs structure of the library means that the outer walls don't have to hold the floors up. Large panes of glass surround the entire library. They let in a lot of light.

Each windowpane was put in place using machine-operated suction cups. After a pane of glass was attached to the suction cups, a crane lifted it into place. Workers then fastened each window to the building.

Even though the windows don't hold up the library's floors, they still have to be strong. Minnesota gets a lot of severe weather, such as thunderstorms and blizzards. The windows have to resist these storms.

Each strip of suction cups can hold about 1,500 pounds. That's the same weight as seventeen ten-year-olds!

Engineers tested a model of the windows in Miami, Florida. The model was exactly like the glass that would be used in Minneapolis. The engineers applied heat and cold. They even set up an airplane engine and propeller to blow air and water at the windows. This was like a rainstorm with 60-mile-per-hour winds. While the engine blew, engineers stood on the other side of the glass. They made sure it didn't crack or leak.

Many of the windows have designs, called etchings, on them. They are images of trees, snow, water, and prairie grass. These images connect the library to the Minnesota landscape.

The etchings also help protect books and readers from the strong summer sun. The process used to make the patterns on the glass is called fritting. Fritting was first developed in Persia (modern Iran) in the Middle East.

The glass for the library's windows
is between ¼ inch and ½ inch thick.

prairie grass

trees

snow

water

A GREAT STEEL WING

Once the building itself was standing, it was time to put on the roof. The library's top is made of several parts, just like the rest of the building. One of its most striking parts is the steel section above Library Commons. This part of the roof sticks out from the building and is supported only at its base, like a diving board. This style is called cantilevering. One of the cantilevered "wings" is 58 feet long and weighs 90 tons. It juts out over Hennepin Avenue, where people pass underneath every day.

From end to end, the library's cantilevered roof is 360 feet long.

The huge metal cantilevered wing was constructed on the ground. It took about a month to build. When workers were ready to lift it 100 feet into the air and attach it to the building, the city closed down the street. Two giant cranes took more than an hour to slowly lift the roof into place. The weight had to be evenly distributed between the cranes at all times, or the cranes would have collapsed or dropped the roof. Workers hustled through the night to line up the wing and get it bolted down. The cantilevered roof makes the building unique. It's as if the library is jutting out its chin proudly, looking toward the future.

More than 100 metal bolts keep the wing fastened to the library.

Behind the Scenes
Steelworker

Construction work runs in Terrance Roy Jr.'s family.

His Native American father and grandfather were also steelworkers. Terrance has worked on buildings all over the country, including the IDS tower in Minneapolis and Bank One Ballpark, where the Arizona Diamondbacks play. He gets a real thrill out of running along the tops of skyscrapers. His friends have told him he must be part monkey because heights don't scare him. He said that the new Central Library

"is the coolest building I've ever worked on."

Terrance's job was to mold and weld much of the steel that holds the library together. The hardest part was the curtain wall. Steel walkways rest against the curtain wall's windows. Since the curtain wall hangs at an angle, the steel walkways each had to be perfectly placed. Terrance called it "a real mental challenge."

Terrance is a big reader, and he has belonged to a book club for twelve years. He wants to start a new book club for Native American kids. As for the downtown library, he said, "I'll spend a lot of time here when it's done."

The new library is also looking toward the future with its rooftop garden. It is planted with shrubs and prairie grass. Because the rooftop has lots of green plants, it is called a green roof. It looks nice, and it's good for the environment. The roof helps keep the library from getting too hot in the summer or too cold in the winter. That means the library spends less money and uses less energy keeping the building the right temperature.

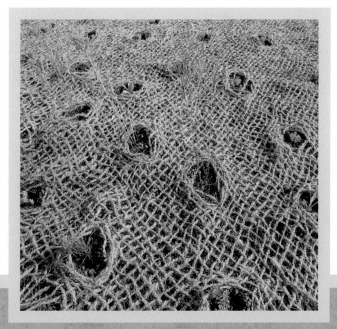

The library is the first public building in Minneapolis to have a green roof. It is 18,560 square feet.

Under the cantilevered roof hangs Teen Central. This area is just for teenagers. The architects got advice from a teen council before they planned this section. Teen Central has books, CDs, DVDs, games, and other materials teens like. It's surrounded by glass and suspended above Hennepin Avenue. This area has one of the best views in the whole building!

The library has more than 38 miles of shelving. But only Teen Central has red, curved bookshelves.

The library also has a separate Children's Library. It's designed in bright colors. The children's section has exhibits that tell about special books or explain things, such as how a caterpillar turns into a butterfly. Colorful structures that look like trees and bridges decorate the Children's Library. Walking through this area is like growing up. First comes the section for toddlers. Then come books for young grade-schoolers. Then, finally, the floor drops down a bit for the section for fifth and sixth graders.

Libraries are great places for students of all ages. You can get help with homework, browse for books, check out new music, and use the computers. The new Central Library also has wireless Internet access. Patrons can surf the Web from their own laptops.

Many libraries offer homework help. In Minneapolis, libraries have tutors to help kids of all ages.

EYES ON THE STARS

Cities have lots of light. Light shines from skyscrapers, from streetlights, and from the houses of all the people who live nearby. Sometimes the lights look sparkly and colorful. But they have a downside too. The glow of the city makes it difficult to view the stars and planets in the night sky. Maybe you've noticed that the stars in rural areas are much brighter than stars in big cities. That's because we see lit objects—especially those far, far away—most clearly when we're standing in the dark.

The good news is that people won't have to go all the way to the country to see the stars. Just like the old Minneapolis libraries, the new Central Library will have

The sun is the closest star to Earth. It is about 93 million miles away.

a planetarium. But building the planetarium started later than construction did for the rest of the building. The planetarium will not open until at least 2009.

The new planetarium's dome will sit at the very top of the library's north wing. The Minnesota Planetarium and Space Discovery Center will hold several science theaters and exhibits. It will be a monument to discovery—just like the library itself. Visitors will be able to look through telescopes at real images of outer space, even during the day.

The planetarium's dome will be 60 feet across. That's about the same as the distance between home plate and the pitcher's mound in professional baseball.

FINISHING TOUCHES

With its cement pillars, limestone, many windows, and cantilevered roof in place, the new library was shaping up. But what about the inside? Walls and roofs, after all, are not the parts that matter most. It's great if a library looks good on the outside, but it must also be fun and easy to use.

The new library's interior design is warm and welcoming. Planners chose maple, a hard light-colored wood, for the walls. They picked out brightly colored carpeting to make the inside more energetic. And they chose comfortable furniture and gas fireplaces. Fireplaces are another Minnesota touch. They're cozy on cold winter days when the snow falls outside.

Construction of the new Central Library officially began on May 20, 2003. It took three years and many, many workers to finish the new building.

The building has many pipes, vents, and wires hidden beneath its floors. The floors are made of raised tiles. An open space underneath the tiles has room for the library's water supply, sprinkler system, and computer cables. Building the floors this way added to the building's flexibility. If the wiring ever needs to be changed, workers can just lift up the tiles.

The library's heating system is also under the tiles. Heat moves up into the library through tiny holes. Hot air naturally rises, so this is a very smart way to heat a building. This way of heating saves money and energy. After the floor panels and carpeting were ready, workers put up the maple walls and finished the four gas fireplaces.

The library's heating system includes special blowers near the windows. Without the blowers, the glass might fog up when it's cold outside.

The library hired artists to create pieces of art to hang above each fireplace. Libraries include art in their buildings for a few different reasons. First, it's fun to look at. But art also gets us thinking about new ideas.

One special art piece can only be seen when the library's main elevators move. People in Library Commons can watch two glass elevator cars go up and down. Letters appear on the cars. The letters spell out words as the cars move. The letters are made of light-emitting diodes (LEDs), the same kind of lights you find in digital clocks and watches. The words come from the library's computers. For example, the LEDs may show the title of a book somebody just checked out.

Seven artists created works for the new library. Ben Rubin of New York City designed "Four Stories," the electronic light sculpture for the elevators.

Even though the library looks new and modern, the designers didn't forget about its past. They kept an old mantel—decorative wood or stone around a fireplace—from the first downtown library. It forms a doorway arch on the fourth floor. That doorway is the entrance to the new library's rare book collection.

The architects found a new place for Minerva too. She got a good cleaning before she moved to the new library. She stands at the bottom of an escalator in Library Commons.

The Library's special collections includes rare books.
Special collections holds more than 25,000 items.

As the library's interior was finished, the furniture showed up. Some of the furniture had to be specially made. Workers hauled in desks and chairs. They brought in more than 300 computers. They lugged in long reading tables where lots of people can sit together. At first, designers had wanted smaller tables. But they decided that larger tables would let more people meet one another. Finally came the most important furniture of all—the bookshelves.

Some areas have compact shelving. These shelves hold twice as many books as ordinary bookshelves. They sit on tracks and slide from side to side when someone needs a specific book. The shelves are electric, and they move at the flip of a switch. The builders had to plan carefully for these shelves—since they hold twice as many books, the floor below them has to support twice as much weight!

The library's current collection stands at more than 2 million items. If the novels alone were laid end to end, they would stretch for 18 miles!

Everybody was eager to move the books into the new library. Most of the books had been in storage at a huge warehouse. Others came from a temporary library that was open during construction. The workers finished the library from the ground up. They started by shelving the books on the first floor and worked their way to the top. Putting all the books on the shelves took about four months!

The library also added many new items. With nearly $500,000 in donations, the library bought books, DVDs, and other materials. They called this their opening day collection. With the new books added to the old ones, the downtown Minneapolis library has the fourth-largest collection of any central library in the country.

Once the library was finished, it was time for the people to come. On May 20, 2006, the library officially opened its doors.

All the signs at the library are in four languages: English, Spanish, Hmong, and Somali. These are some of the most common languages spoken in Minneapolis.

COME ONE, COME ALL

You might think that because so many people have computers at home, libraries are not as important as they used to be. But libraries continue to thrive. More people use libraries than ever. The Minneapolis library system, including its branch libraries, has twenty thousand visitors every day. About 80 percent of Minneapolis children have library cards.

Hundreds and even thousands of years ago, libraries were mostly private. Usually only rich people, kings, and religious leaders could use them. Books were copied by hand. They were so expensive that they were sometimes chained to the shelves. But the invention of the printing press changed everything. More books became available, and many copies could be printed. More people attended school and learned how to read. In the United States, the first free libraries opened in the 1800s.

This library is at Hereford Cathedral in Great Britain. It began in the year 1100. Can you guess why it's called a chained library?

The best thing about public libraries—besides the many materials you can get there—is that anybody can use them. That includes children and teenagers, college students, working people, and people looking for work. The information people find in books tends to be more in-depth than what's on the Internet. Looking at a computer screen for a long time can make your eyes tired.

In an average year, the Minneapolis Public Library system circulates 3 million items and welcomes 1.6 million visitors.

Besides, at the library, you get the benefit of librarians. Librarians are specially trained to answer questions. They are friendly and know where to find things. They can tell sources of trustworthy information from sources that might not be trustworthy. It's very difficult to stump a librarian. Just try, and you'll find out.

Libraries also have resources for people who have just moved to the United States. Many people in Minneapolis and Saint Paul speak languages other than English. They may speak Hmong, Vietnamese, Chinese, Somali, Russian, or Spanish. The new library has special areas stocked with newspapers, books, and even computers with home pages written in foreign languages. These resources help immigrants find jobs. They can also keep track of news from their hometowns. The library offers tutoring to help immigrants get comfortable in their new surroundings.

Reference librarians across the United States answer more than 7 million questions a week.

Behind the Scenes
Librarian

For Marcelyn Sletten, the best thing about being a librarian is answering the questions people ask. "They will never fail to surprise you with what they come up with," said Marcelyn. She has been a librarian for ten years.

Marcelyn loves working with the library's many books. She said she never has enough time to read all the books she would like. Still, she would rather read than watch television or use the computer. Some of her favorite books are about architecture.

Marcelyn works in the children's section of the downtown Minneapolis library. She enjoys talking with kids because they are so excited about reading. "We have a lot of kids, even really small four year olds, who have a strong interest in dinosaurs," she said. "We have six-year-olds interested in forensic pathology, germs, and stuff." Marcelyn can find just the right book on any subject.

A book can change your life with ideas, she said. "There's something about the printed word, the experience of it, that's really different from the computer." Plus, you can take a book to the beach!

You may have heard of Andrew Carnegie. At the age of twelve, he moved with his family from Scotland to Pennsylvania. The family was very poor. In the United States, he had to get a job in a mill instead of going to school. But Andrew wanted to learn. He found a small library and read books whenever he could. Later in life, Carnegie became very rich in the steel industry. But he never forgot the importance of reading. He used his money to help build thousands of libraries in the late 1800s and early 1900s. Most of them are in the United States and Great Britain.

Carnegie supported libraries because he believed they would help young people everywhere succeed in life. He said that books held the "chief treasures of the world."

Carnegie funded about 3,000 libraries around the world. Carnegie libraries are in every U.S. state except Alaska, Delaware, and Rhode Island.

Even if you don't plan to become a steel industry millionaire, the library is a great place. Whether you're looking for books, Internet access, or even if you just want to watch people from all walks of life, **come to the library!**

Glossary

ARCHITECT: a person who creates the plans for making houses, buildings, and other structures. The architect is often in charge of the construction.

ASPHALT: a black substance used to make roads

ASTRONOMY: the scientific study of stars, planets, and outer space

BINDERY: a place for making new books or repairing damaged books

BLUEPRINT: a detailed construction plan

BRANCH LIBRARY: a library other than the main, or central, library in a system

CANTILEVERED: a beam or structure that sticks out at one end and is secured at the other, like a diving board

CATALOG: a list of all the books in the library. Catalogs used to be written on cards and stored in drawers, but most modern library catalogs are electronic.

CEMENT: a building material made from concrete, gravel, sand, and water

CITY COUNCIL: an elected group that serves as the legislative branch of city government

architect

bindery

cement

CURTAIN WALL: an outer wall of a building that does not bear any weight

ENGINEER: a person who is trained to design buildings, bridges, and other structures

FICTION: stories about characters and events that are made up by an author

LIGHT-EMITTING DIODES (LEDs): electronic devices that light up when electricity passes through them

LIMESTONE: a hard rock used in building

MINERVA: the Roman goddess of wisdom

NONFICTION: stories or writing about true people, places, and things

PATRON: anyone who uses a library

PLANETARIUM: a building that projects images of the stars, planets, moons, and other parts of the universe onto a large, curved ceiling

RECYCLE: to reuse old objects

SLAB: a broad, flat piece of something, such as cement

engineer

LED

patron

LIBRARY RESOURCES

Finding your local library isn't very hard. You can ask your parents or a teacher where to find a library, you can look up *library* in the phone book, or you can use one of these websites.

LIBRARY LOCATOR

http://nces.ed.gov/nceskids/library/
This site has a map of the United States. You can click on your state to find a list of all the cities with public libraries. When you click on the name of a specific library, you get the address, phone number, and a few extra fun facts.

PUBLIC LIBRARIES

http://www.publiclibraries.com
Find the name of your state on this website, and get the names of all the public library systems in your state. When you click on the name of a library, you'll be connected directly to its website.

YOUR OWN LIBRARY WEBSITE

Once you find the website for your library, bookmark it so that you always know where to find it. Your library's website will tell you where to find nearby libraries, when they are open, and how to get a library card. In some states, a card for one library will let you check out books from any library in the whole state. You may need a parent or other adult with you when you sign up for your library card.

You can also use the online catalog to look up books, movies, or CDs ahead of time. You can renew whatever you've checked out, make a request, or even ask for

KITCHIGAMI
P.O. Box 84, Pine River.
..nesota 56474

Serving
• Beltrami • Cass
• Crow Wing • Hubbard
• Wadena counties
with libraries i..
• Bem..

CITY OF SAINT PAUL
PUBLIC LIBRARY

Renewals...............651-292-6002
Information..........651-266-7000
http://www.stpaul.lib.mn.us
This is a MELSA Library

..dison Public Library

..al - 266-6300
..V. Mifflin St.
..horne
..E. Washington Ave.
..iew
..N. Sherman Ave.
..owridge
..Raymond Rd.

Monroe Street
1705 Monroe St.
Pinney
204 Cottage Grove Rd.
Sequoya
513 S. Midvale Blvd.
South Madi..

A member of
..s card may be used at an..

HENNEPIN COUNTY LIBRARY
www.hclib.org
TOMORROW'S LIBRARY...

an Interlibrary Loan (ILL). When your library doesn't have the book, CD, or movie you want, you can get an ILL. This means that another library will send the item to your library so that you can check it out. Sometimes you might get an ILL from halfway across the country. And best of all, ILLs are free!

Source Notes

5 Germaine Greer, *Daddy, We Hardly Knew You* (New York: Knopf, 1989), 70.

13 Bruce Weir Benidt, *The Library Book* (Minneapolis: Minneapolis Public Library and Information Center, 1984), 154.

16 Barb Johnson, in discussion with the author, July 2005.

18 "Minneapolis Library in Good Company," *libraryjournal.com*, June 1, 2005, http://www.libraryjournal.com/article/CA602654.html (September 13, 2005).

23 Nina Ebbighausen, in discussion with the author, July 2005.

38 Terrance Roy Jr., in discussion with the author, July 2005.

53 Marcelyn Sletten, in discussion with the author, July 2005.

54 Mary Goljenboom, "How Waukegan Got Its Carnegie Library," *cppi.org*, http://www.cppi.org/Building_history.html (August 10, 2005).

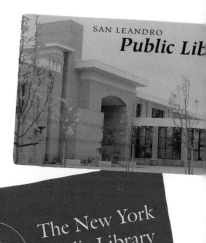

Selected Bibliography

Battles, Matthew. *Library: An Unquiet History.* New York: W. W. Norton, 2003.

Benidt, Bruce Weir. *The Library Book.* Minneapolis: Minneapolis Public Library and Information Center, 1984.

Pelli, Cesar and Associates. *Minneapolis Central Library Schematic Design.* New Haven, CT: Cesar Pelli & Associates, 2002.

Further Reading and Websites

American Library Association

http://www.ala.org

The American Library Association is a national organization for libraries and librarians. Its website includes information about improving funding for libraries and making sure communities know about the importance of libraries.

The Carnegie Corporation

http://www.carnegie.org/sub/kids/index.html

This is the site of the charitable foundation Andrew Carnegie established. It features a special section for kids with a timeline, information about libraries, photo gallery, and more.

Dewey Decimal System

http://www.lib.duke.edu/libguide/fi_books_dd_list.htm

The Duke University Libraries run this website that explains how the Dewey decimal system works.

Edge, Laura B. *Andrew Carnegie: Industrial Philanthropist.* Minneapolis: Lerner
   Publications Company, 2004.
   Learn about Andrew Carnegie's life, including his childhood in Scotland, his early
   jobs in the United States, and his successful career as a leader in the steel and
   railroad industries.

Fowler, Allan. *The Dewey Decimal System.* New York: Children's Press, 1996.
   This book breaks down the Dewey decimal system and explains how libraries use
   it to organize books.

———. *The Library of Congress.* New York: Children's Press, 1996.
   Find out how the Library of Congress was created.

Hill, Lee Sullivan. *Libraries Take Us Far.* Minneapolis: Carolrhoda Books, Inc., 1998.
   This book tells about the history of libraries and has photographs of libraries all
   across the United States.

Laubier, Guillaume de. *The Most Beautiful Libraries in the World.* New York: Abrams,
   2003.
   This photo book features stunning libraries from around the world.

THE LIBRARY COMPANY OF PHILADELPHIA
   http://www.librarycompany.org/
   Read about the Library Company of Philadelphia, founded in 1731 by
   Benjamin Franklin. It is a research library focusing on American culture and
   history from the colonial period through the nineteenth century.

THE LIBRARY OF CONGRESS

http://www.loc.gov

Find out all about the world's largest library. This site includes a special section for kids and families.

MINNEAPOLIS PUBLIC LIBRARY

http://www.mplib.org

The website for the Minneapolis Public Library has information about the construction of the new Central Library, the history of Minneapolis, and everything you need to know about the library system.

Raatma, Lucia. *Libraries.* New York: Children's Press, 1998.

Learn about the history of libraries and books, from ancient times to the present.

THE RICHEST MAN IN THE WORLD: ANDREW CARNEGIE

http://www.pbs.org/wgbh/amex/carnegie/

Special features on this site include virtual tours of Carnegie mansions and a look at the steel and railroad business.

Simon, Charnan. *Andrew Carnegie: Builder of Libraries.* New York: Children's Press, 1997.

Find out the story of Andrew Carnegie's life and why he gave so much money to libraries.

Wilcox, Charlotte. *A Skyscraper Story.* Minneapolis: Carolrhoda Books, Inc., 1990.

This book tells the story of the construction of another building designed by Cesar Pelli—the Norwest Center in Minneapolis, Minnesota.

INDEX

ABOUT THE AUTHOR

Jennifer Vogel was born in Minneapolis, Minnesota, but has also lived in Seattle, Washington, and briefly, Oaxaca, Mexico. She graduated from the University of Minnesota with a degree in journalism. She worked for years as a writer and investigative reporter for *City Pages*, an alternative weekly in Minneapolis, and a range of local and national magazines and newspapers. She also served as editor in chief of *The Stranger*, a weekly newspaper in Seattle. In 2004, she published *Flim-Flam Man*, a memoir about her father, which won the Minnesota Book Award.

PHOTO ACKNOWLEDGMENTS

The images in this book are used with the permission of: Courtesy Charles Gimon/Minneapolis Public Library, construction sequence on endsheets; Courtesy Pelli Clarke Pelli Architects, pp. 2, 42, 51 (main), 55; © Peter Freed, p. 6; © Dan Marshall, p. 7; © Digital Art/CORBIS, p. 8; Courtesy Library Project Office, pp. 9, 25 (all), 32 (both), 33 (both), 36 (left), 37, 39 (left), 43 (both), 56 (right), 57 (center); Courtesy Minneapolis Public Library, Minneapolis Collection, pp. 10 (both), 11 (left), 12 (right), 13, 15 (top); Star Tribune/Minneapolis-St. Paul 2006 provided by Minneapolis Public Library, Minneapolis Collection, p. 11 (right); Library of Congress, pp. 12 left (LC-USZC4-7214), 54 (LC-USZ62-120152); NASA, p. 14 (both); © Todd Strand/Independent Picture Service, pp. 15 (bottom), 17 (bottom), 19, 20, 21, 22 (both), 23 (left), 24, 26 (all), 27 (right), 28, 29, 30, 31, 34 (trees and grass), 35, 36 (right), 38, 39 (right), 40 (both), 41 (both), 44, 45, 47, 48, 49, 51 (insets), 52, 53, 56 (center), 57 (left), 61, 63, 64, 65; © Kathleen Lamb, p. 16; Thomas Cooper Library, Rare Books & Special Collections, University of South Carolina, p. 17 (top); BECAUSE OF WINN-DIXIE Copyright © 2000 Kate DiCamillo. Cover illustration Copyright © 2000 Chris Sheban. Reprinted by permission of the publisher Candlewick Press, Inc., p. 17 (middle); © JIMIN LAI/AFP/Getty Images, p. 18; Courtesy Aaron Mullins and Architectural Alliance, pp. 23 (right), 56 (left); © Bettmann/CORBIS, p. 27 (inset); © Danielle Carnito/Independent Picture Service, pp. 34 (snow and water), background image throughout; © Ben Rubin/EAR Studio, p. 46; © Jarrold Publishing, p. 50; © Royalty-Free/CORBIS, p. 57 (right).

Front cover: Courtesy Pelli Clarke Pelli Architects